STRETCH
to the Sun

From a Tiny Sprout
to the Tallest Tree
on Earth

Carrie A. Pearson

Illustrated by
Susan Swan

Charlesbridge

To all the trees I've climbed, read books in, and rested beneath.
And to my parents, who showed me the importance of nature.—C. A. P.

For the very tall Terry and the newest family members, not very tall yet,
but growing fast: Zander and Elise Rasberry and James Canon Feazell.—S. S.

Published by Charlesbridge
85 Main Street
Watertown, MA 02472
(617) 926-0329
www.charlesbridge.com

Library of Congress Cataloging-in-Publication Data
Names: Pearson, Carrie A., 1962– author. | Swan, Susan, 1944– illustrator.
Title: Stretch to the sun: from a tiny sprout to the tallest tree on earth/
    Carrie A. Pearson; illustrated by Susan Swan.
Description: Watertown, MA: Charlesbridge, [2018]
Identifiers: LCCN 2018005806 (print) | LCCN 2018007178 (ebook) |
    ISBN 9781632896315 (ebook) | ISBN 9781632896322 (ebook pdf) |
    ISBN 9781580897716 (reinforced for library use)
Subjects: LCSH: Redwoods—California—Juvenile literature. | Redwood
    National Park (Calif.)—Juvenile literature.
Classification: LCC SD397.R3 (ebook) | LCC SD397.R3 P36 2018 (print) |
    DDC 634.9/75809794—dc23
LC record available at https://lccn.loc.gov/2018005806

Printed in China
(hc) 10 9 8 7 6 5 4 3 2 1

Illustrations created by manipulating found objects, hand-painted papers, and scans of
    objects and textures in Adobe Photoshop to create new patterns; adding digital
    paintings; and then collaging the two together
Display type set in Herschel Creamline by Brian Brubaker, Amatic Bold by Vernon Adams,
    Alina by Mika Melvas, and Chicken Basket by Font Diner
Text type set in Myriad Pro by Adobe Systems Incorporated
Color separations by Colourscan Print Co Pte Ltd, Singapore
Printed by 1010 Printing International Limited in Huizhou, Guangdong, China
Production supervision by Brian G. Walker
Designed by Diane M. Earley

Ferocious winter winds blow through a forest of coast redwood trees.

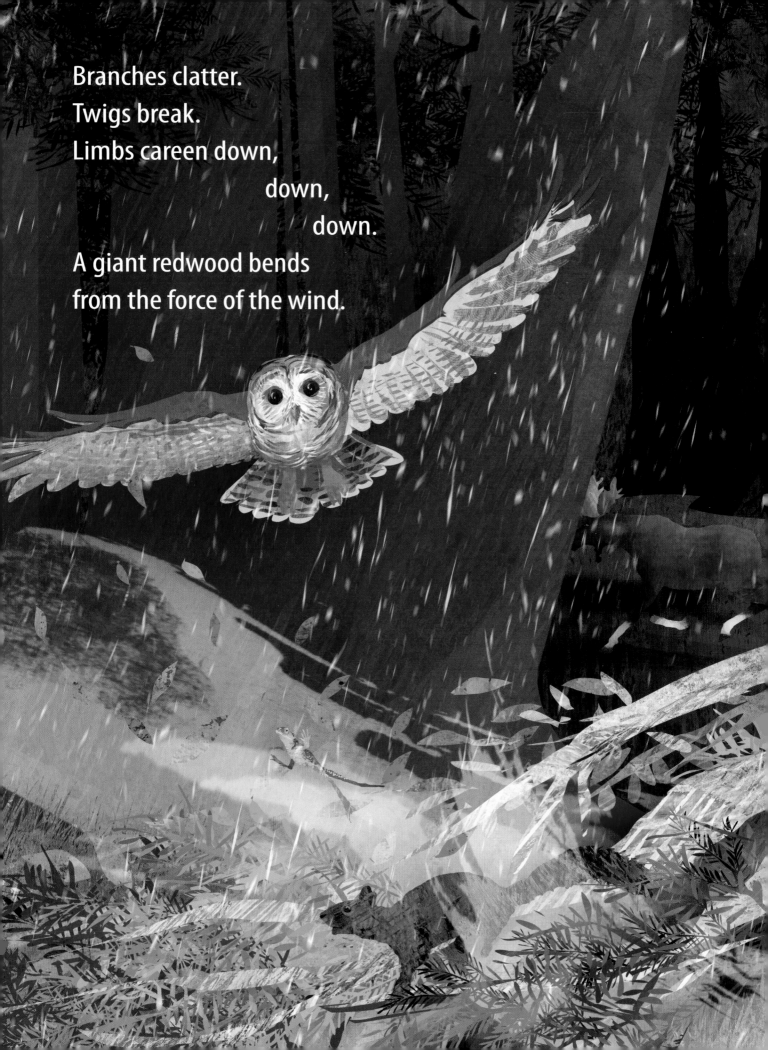

Branches clatter.
Twigs break.
Limbs careen down,
down,
down.
A giant redwood bends
from the force of the wind.

The giant tree falls, broken,
and the forest floor trembles.
Clods of dirt and chunks of wood
fly hundreds of feet.

Then . . . quiet.
Just a whisper of wind.
Just a rustle of leaves.
Just a chirp from a bird.
Then the sound of rain *drip, drip, dripping*
on the ground for months.
Until dewy spring air wakes the forest and . . .

POP! A tiny tree,
no bigger than a pinky finger,
sprouts from the stump of the fallen tree.
The sprout needs light, so it stretches toward the sun.
The sprout needs water, so it reaches out thin roots
to pull moisture from the damp duff.

Autumn leaves drop to the ground,
decay, and help create soil.
Then cold winter rain drizzles
on the leaves and soaks the forest floor.

Spring bees visit, helping to create
more plants to protect the sprout's roots.
Heavy summer fog supplies moisture.
When the sun shines through,
larger trees shield the tiny one.

Every season, every year, just enough light
and just enough water feed the sprout
until six hundred years later . . .

. . . it isn't so little anymore.

Intertwining roots pull moisture inside the tree,
where it travels up, up, up to the tippy top,
more than two hundred feet high.

At the tree's crown, branches form platforms
that collect leaves, bark, and smaller limbs.
The debris turns to soil.
Birds and animals visit the tree
and drop seeds in that soil.

Now huckleberry bushes and ferns inch toward the sky.
Lichens and mosses make blankets over the branches.
Wandering salamanders hide in cool notches.
Northern flying squirrels soar from limb to limb.

Marbled murrelet birds feed their chicks
in mossy hollows two hundred feet high.
Branches crisscross with other giants and
form a canopy—a unique, wondrous world.
The once-tiny tree grows taller each season.

One day the sky darkens. Rain pours and . . .
a bolt of lightning rips through the clouds
and strikes the ground near the tree.

CRACK!

HISS!

SIZZLE!

ROAR!

Fire engulfs the area, destroying many trees.
But the once-tiny tree's bark is so thick
that it survives with only black scars.

The tree grows taller still.

For hundreds of years
the tree is busy with life,
but the forest is quiet. Until . . .
not deer,
not cougar,
not black bear.

CRUNCH!

RUSTLE!

STOMP!

Horse hooves and human footsteps.
People scout the forest for trees to harvest
for lumber as soon as good roads are built.
Without roads there's no harvesting. Not yet.

Decades later good roads are built—near the tree.
Powerful yellow lights pierce the night.
Not starlight.
Not moonlight.
Not light from the aurora borealis.
Flashlights and headlights.
Exhaust clouds the air
as saws carve through
huge trunks.

The tangy, sharp scent of cut evergreen
mixes with bitter fumes.
The ground near the once-tiny tree
shudders as other ancient redwoods crash.
Tractors haul trees out of the forest,
crushing everything in their paths.

But soon, across the country in Washington, DC,
people listen to a different sound—pen on paper.
The pen is held by the president of the United States
as he signs a law protecting ancient trees.

The loud noises stop
as suddenly as they started.
Protected from harvest,
the tree grows older and taller.

One day . . .
humble voices,
measuring tapes,
camera clicks.

Explorers look for tall trees
all over the world,
and here they find one.
At 379.1 feet, it is the
tallest one ever discovered.

Scientists study the once-tiny sprout
that survived and grew to be . . .

THE TALLEST OF THE TALL.

AUTHOR'S NOTE

This book began with a question. My mother asked me, "Do you know what's going on in the tops of redwood trees?" She had watched a documentary about the tallest tree ever found and thought I'd be interested. I watched it, and she was right! I knew children would want to learn about the tallest tree species in the world. First I researched the topic by reading books from the library and using the internet. When I knew what questions to ask, I began primary research by contacting tall-tree scientists and researchers.

Then I received a grant from the Society of Children's Book Writers and Illustrators (SCBWI) to travel from my home in Michigan to Redwood National Park in California. James B. Wheeler, a park ranger and interpreter for the National Park Service for more than thirty years, was my guide. He shared his knowledge of and love for coast redwoods. Later he reviewed several drafts of the manuscript and provided expert information. My inspiration grew from his words: "Every tree has a story to tell."

FACTS ABOUT COAST REDWOODS

A tiny tree, no bigger than a pinky finger, sprouts from the stump of the fallen tree.
We don't know if the tree in this book came from a seed or a sprout. New coast redwood trees can grow from seeds that trees produce or from sprouts that emerge from the base of a stump, a fallen branch, or a **burl** (a rounded knot on the tree with dormant buds). More trees grow from sprouts because seeds aren't released every year, and it takes the right conditions for them to grow. If the tree in this book did come from a sprout, it means that every one of its cells is a perfect copy—a clone—of the original tree.

The sprout needs water, so it reaches out thin roots to pull moisture from the damp duff.
When fallen leaves, sticks, and plants decay, a rich layer of organic matter called **duff** is created. Duff absorbs water like a sponge and provides crucial moisture for the tree's roots.

At the tree's crown, branches form platforms that collect leaves, bark, and smaller limbs.
When branches or trunks break off, coast redwoods grow new ones. This is called **reiteration** and is an important part of how redwood trees survive for hundreds and sometimes thousands of years.

Branches crisscross with other giants and form a canopy—a unique, wondrous world.
The **canopy** is the top layer in a forest where the crowns of trees overlap. In a redwood forest, the canopy is very high off the ground, and until scientists found a way to climb using ropes and pulleys, no one knew what was up there. Research began at Humboldt State University in 1996 with the work of Stephen Sillett, Scott Sillett, and Marie Antoine. What they found was astonishing. Northern flying squirrels live in cracks or holes in the trees. They spread the thin skin between their legs to trap air and then float from tree to tree. Wandering salamanders are amphibians that live and breed in canopy soils and in cracks in tree bark. They do not have lungs and must keep their skin moist to breathe, so they come out only when the air is full of moisture. Marbled murrelets, an endangered bird species, nest in coast redwoods and feed on fish from the nearby Pacific Ocean. Canopy plants and lichens like *Leproloma membranacea* provide food for the many insect species that live far above the ground.

For hundreds of years the tree is busy with life, but the forest is quiet.

Thousands of years before the tree in this book sprouted, coast redwood (*Sequoia sempervirens*) forests grew along the Pacific coast from California to Oregon. Several Native American tribes lived within the forests and used fallen trees for building materials and canoes, but by and large the forests remained undisturbed.

People scout the forest for trees to harvest for lumber as soon as good roads are built.

In 1848 the Gold Rush began, and thousands of people traveled west to seek their fortune. Trees were needed to make houses, boats, and buildings. Coast redwoods provide excellent lumber because they split easily and are fire- and insect-resistant. Over time, redwood was used for railroad cars and ties, coffins, water and wine vats, water pipes, furniture, shingles, window frames, doors, bridges, decks, wharf pilings, fences, and insulation.

By the late 1800s people recognized that the ancient trees were disappearing quickly. John C. Merriam, Henry Fairfield Osborn, and Madison Grant established the Save the Redwoods League in 1918. The League's mission is still "to protect and restore redwood forests and connect people with their peace and beauty so these wonders of the natural world flourish." The League saved thousands of trees by purchasing land on which they grew, but sadly, millions more were not on protected land.

Timber cruisers traveled through the thick woods (sometimes on horseback), selected trees to harvest, and marked them with paint. (This paint still can be seen on some trees today.) Loggers followed with axes, chains, and saws. Oxen, horses, and mules pulled trees out of the forest to **flumes** (water-filled ditches), rivers, or railcars. The trees eventually made it to lumber mills. When redwood harvesting began in the mid-1800s, there were more than two million acres of old-growth redwood forests. By 1968 nine out of ten trees were gone forever.

But soon, across the country in Washington, DC, people listen to a different sound— pen on paper.

After many years negotiating with the timber industry, the US Congress created Redwood National Park on October 2, 1968, which placed tens of thousands of acres in the care of the National Park Service. Then in 1978, as modern-day loggers worked around the clock to harvest timber, President Jimmy Carter signed a law that expanded Redwood National Park by another 48,000 acres.

Today fewer than 120,000 acres of old-growth coast redwoods remain. The National Park Service, the Save the Redwoods League, the Sempervirens Fund, and many other organizations and individuals continue to work on behalf of coast redwoods.

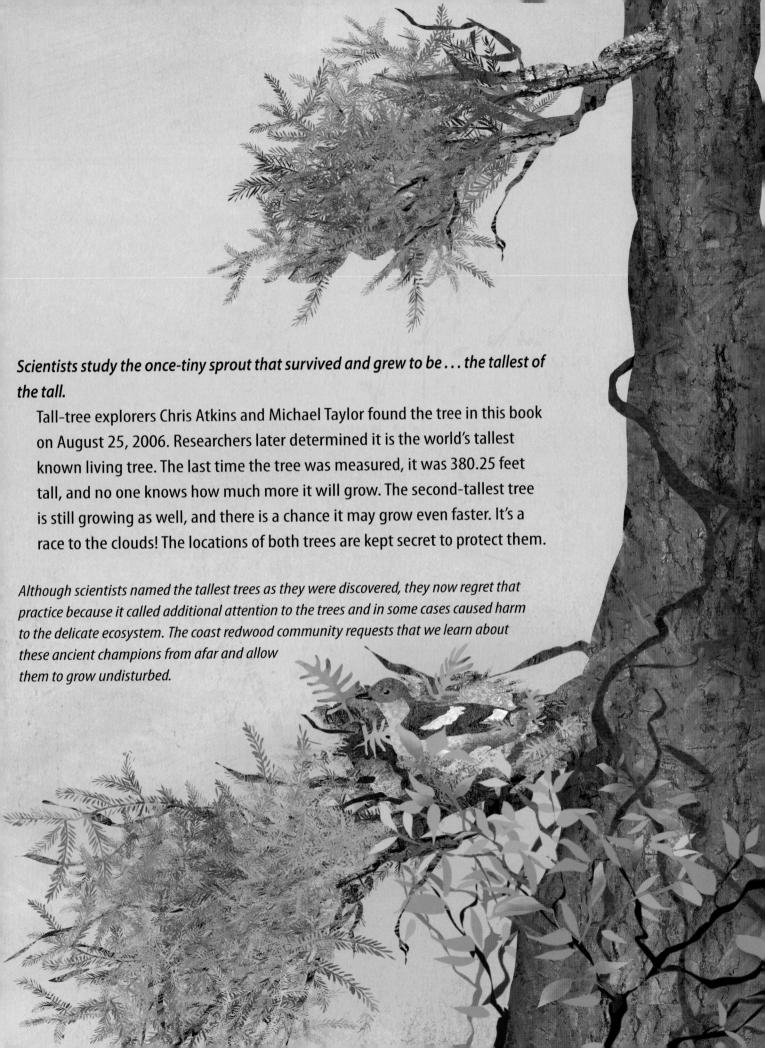

Scientists study the once-tiny sprout that survived and grew to be . . . the tallest of the tall.

Tall-tree explorers Chris Atkins and Michael Taylor found the tree in this book on August 25, 2006. Researchers later determined it is the world's tallest known living tree. The last time the tree was measured, it was 380.25 feet tall, and no one knows how much more it will grow. The second-tallest tree is still growing as well, and there is a chance it may grow even faster. It's a race to the clouds! The locations of both trees are kept secret to protect them.

Although scientists named the tallest trees as they were discovered, they now regret that practice because it called additional attention to the trees and in some cases caused harm to the delicate ecosystem. The coast redwood community requests that we learn about these ancient champions from afar and allow them to grow undisturbed.

Selected Bibliography

Barbour, Michael G., John Evarts, Marjorie Popper, Valerie Whitworth, Sandy Lydon, and
    Mark Borchert. *Coast Redwood: A Natural and Cultural History*. Los Olivos, CA: Cachuma, 2001.

Bearss, Edwin C. "The Lumber Industry 1850–1953." *Redwood National Park History: Basic Data: Del Norte and
    Humboldt Counties, California*. US Department of the Interior, National Park Service, Division of History,
    Office of Archeology and Historic Preservation, 1982. https://www.nps.gov/parkhistory/online_books/redw/.

Burns, Steve. *Climbing Redwood Giants*. DVD. Washington, DC: National Geographic, 2009. 50 min.

Martin, Glen. "Humboldt County / World's Tallest Tree, a Redwood, Confirmed." *SFGate*, September 29, 2006.
    http://www.sfgate.com/bayarea/article/HUMBOLDT-COUNTY-World-s-tallest-tree-a-2550557.php.

Save the Redwoods League. "Coast Redwoods," 2018. https://www.savetheredwoods.org/redwoods/coast-redwoods/.

National Park Service, US Department of the Interior. "Redwood National and State Parks: Area History." Last modified
    December 7, 2016. https://www.nps.gov/redw/historyculture/area-history.htm#CP_JUMP_66521.

Wheeler, James B. (park ranger/interpreter, National Park Service, US Department of the Interior), personal interview
    by Carrie A. Pearson, August 5, 2014.

Learn More

Visit

- Big Basin Redwoods State Park: Boulder Creek, California
- Del Norte Coast Redwoods State Park: seven miles south of Crescent City, California
- Humboldt Redwoods State Park: Weott, California
- Jedediah Smith Redwoods State Park: nine miles east of Crescent City, California
- Prairie Creek Redwoods State Park: Humboldt County near Orick, California
- Redwood National and State Parks: Crescent City, California

Who Helps?

- *Redwood National and State Parks* protect the tallest trees on earth, educate people about their importance, and create experiences within forests. https://www.nps.gov/redw/index.htm
- *Redwood Parks Conservancy* provides visitor services and educational programs and supports important projects within the Redwood National and State Parks. https://redwoodparksconservancy.org
- *Save the Redwoods League* protects and restores redwood forests and land, studies habitats, and creates partnerships that help forests survive. https://www.savetheredwoods.org
- *Sempervirens Fund* is California's oldest land trust and protects the redwood forests of the Santa Cruz Mountains. https://sempervirens.org

How Can You Help?

- Hug a tree at a national or state park!
- Visit a visitor center and learn!
- Become a citizen scientist!
- Dedicate a tree in honor of someone you love!

Online

Watch world tall-tree expert Dr. Stephen Sillett climb, learn about, and measure the tallest tree ever discovered.
    http://news.nationalgeographic.com/news/2007/01/070123-redwoods-video.html

Check out activities and Redwood EdVentures at the National and State Parks Service children's portal.
    https://www.nps.gov/redw/forkids/index.htm

Visit the Save the Redwoods League Learning Center.
    https://www.savetheredwoods.org/learning-center/

The URLs listed here were accurate at publication, but websites often change.
If a URL doesn't work, you can use the internet to find more information.